This journal belongs to:

"EVERYTHING CAN BE TAKEN FROM A MAN BUT ONE THING: THE LAST OF THE HUMAN FREEDOMS—TO CHOOSE ONE'S ATTITUDE IN ANY GIVEN SET OF CIRCUMSTANCES, TO CHOOSE ONE'S OWN WAY."

Viktor E. Frankl, Auschwitz survivor

Man's Search for Meaning

Dear Reader,

Thanks for purchasing our book.

We feel grateful to serve you with our carefully created:

The Self-Confidence Journal

& Hope you enjoy, learn and find what you're looking for.

All the best,

21 Exercises

As a little thank you note,
*we've three **Free** Personal-Growth exercises waiting for you.*

Simply send an email to to exercises21@yahoo.com
Title the email "Gratitude"

And we will send you Three Personal Development Hacks for Free..

THE SELF-CONFIDENCE JOURNAL

Follow us on Instagram
For promotions, giveaways and newest arrivals

Instagram: 21exercises_journals

The

Self-Confidence Journal

LEARN TO DEAL WITH INSECURITIES &
SOCIAL ANXIETY IN 90 DAYS

Created by:
21 Exercises

True Potential Project 2018

A Message From The Authors

Journaling is a way to better understand life, the people around you and yourself. It's a peaceful exercise that demands us to hold still for a brief moment, escaping clouded Facebook feeds, screaming news channels and daily stress. An ancient exercise, also, to think about life. Recharging your battery. Setting a new direction. And, above all, being conscious, living in the here and now, open to new experiences, able to connect with others and reassured of your ability to cope with (temporary) setbacks.

INTRODUCTION

Self-confidence
/ˌsɛlfˈkɒnfɪd(ə)ns/

noun

A feeling of trust in one's abilities, qualities, and judgement.

Sometimes the dictionary is the perfect way to understand a concept. What better way than describing Self-Confidence as *"A feeling of trust in one's abilities, qualities, and judgement"*. These words project calmness and determination.   Evidently, this feeling, or even this state of self-confidence, is attainable for everyone. It isn't about adding, it is about recognizing yourself as who you truly are.

The different questions and inspirational quotes in this *Self-Confidence Journal* guide you on a journey to gain trust in your abilities, qualities, and judgement. To help you deal better with insecurities, social anxieties, and negative thoughts. Because faith in yourself leads to better actions, the courage to express yourself authentically & the stability to deal with the inevitable challenges of life more grounded. Make this journal your new small habit for the next three months and see the powerful changes for yourself.

How To Use This Journal

On every page, you'll find a new day and a new question. If you bought the print version, there is enough space on each page to answer the daily question and do more journaling. There is a specific order to these *Self-Confidence Journaling* questions, to give you the best benefit. If you bought the EBook version, you could use your own notebook during these 90 days. We recommend setting a particular time each day for you journaling exercises. You could do it during your morning routine, or before you go to bed. See it as a calming & self-improvement exercise that will bring you good results and a better experience of life.

BECAUSE ONE BELIEVES IN ONESELF,
ONE DOESN'T TRY TO CONVINCE OTHERS.

BECAUSE ONE IS CONTENT WITH ONESELF,
ONE DOESN'T NEED OTHERS' APPROVAL.

BECAUSE ONE ACCEPTS ONESELF,
THE WHOLE WORLD ACCEPTS HIM OR HER.

Lao Tzu

Day 1

THERE IS NOTHING IN THE WORLD SO IRRESISTIBLY CONTAGIOUS AS LAUGHTER AND GOOD HUMOR.

Charles Dickens

What qualities do you have, make you stand out from other people?

_____

_____

_____

_____

_____

_____

_____

_____

_____

_____

_____

_____

_____

_____

_____

_____

_____

_____

_____

_____

_____

_____

_____

Day 2

Write down three past experiences where making a mistake actually turned out to be a blessing.

Day 3

Once we believe in ourselves, we can risk curiosity, wonder, spontaneous delight, or any experience that reveals the human spirit.

E.E. Cummings

Write down three recent memories when you felt super self-confident. What can you learn from these experiences?

Day 4

All sins are attempts to fill voids.
Simone Weil

Write down five past achievements that make you proud.

Day 5

But how could you live and have no story to tell?

Fyodor Dostoevsky

In what area in your life do you feel completely certain about yourself and why?

Day 6

Always laugh when you can, it is cheap medicine.

Lord Byron

How could the way you dealt with temporary setbacks in the past, help you in the present and future?

_____

_____

_____

_____

_____

_____

_____

_____

_____

_____

_____

_____

_____

_____

_____

_____

_____

_____

_____

_____

_____

_____

_____

Day 7

Risk anything! Care no more for the opinion of others ... Do the hardest thing on earth for you. Act for yourself. Face the truth.

Katherine Mansfield

What social conditions are restricting you from making the choices you actually want?

Day 8

Angry people are not always wise.

Jane Austen

What is your definition for self-confidence?

_____
_____
_____
_____
_____
_____
_____
_____
_____
_____
_____
_____
_____
_____
_____
_____
_____
_____
_____
_____
_____
_____

Day 9

We may brave human laws, but we cannot resist natural ones.

Jules Verne

Look at yesterday's answer.

What self-confidence qualities do you already have?
And what qualities do you still need to work on?

Day 10

Nothing contributes so much to tranquilize the mind as a steady purpose.

Mary Shelley

What one thing could you do today to help yourself deal better
with insecurities/social anxieties?

_____

_____

_____

_____

_____

_____

_____

_____

_____

_____

_____

_____

_____

_____

_____

_____

_____

_____

_____

_____

_____

_____

Day 11

The enemy is a very good teacher.

The Dalai Lama

Write down in detail what *fear* actually is.

Day 12

**I have said it before,
but I don't think I have ever came so near meaning it.**

Kate Chopin

Write down three things other people can learn from you.

Day 13

I know who I am and who I may be, if I choose.

Miguel de Cervantes Saavedra

Write down three things you can do when the sensation of fear arises.

Day 14

**I have always thought the actions of men
the best interpreters of their thoughts.**

John Locke

Write down everything that makes you feel insecure.

Day 15

It is never too late to be what you might have been.

George Eliot

Look at yesterday's list.
How many of these insecurities are actually based on reality?

Day 16

**Keeping busy and making optimism a way of life
can restore your faith in yourself.**

Lucille Ball

How can optimism help you to be more productive?

_____

_____

_____

_____

_____

_____

_____

_____

_____

_____

_____

_____

_____

_____

_____

_____

_____

_____

_____

_____

_____

_____

Day 17

Attention is the rarest and purest form of generosity.

Simone Weil

For the next three days pay close attention to all the insecurities and social anxieties that arise. In what situations do you feel them? Where in your body do you feel it? What does it do to you to feel these insecurities? What thoughts are coming up exactly? Pick one of these questions, or pick an attention point yourself, and write down your reflections. Shine the spotlight on these thoughts and emotions that paralyzes you.

Day 18

**In the morning there is meaning,
in the evening there is feeling.**

Gertrude Stein

What is your favorite strategy to deal with rejection?
Why do you use this strategy?

Day 19

**Fate leads the willing
and drags along the reluctant.**

Seneca

What people in your life have a negative influence on you?
Why?

Day 20

Everybody gets so much information all day long that they lose their common sense.

Gertrude Stein

Write down three things that motivate you.

Day 21

Fear defeats more people than any other one thing in the world.

Ralph Waldo Emerson

Write down three past experiences where fear
had a deathly grip on your life.

Day 22

**Act as if what you do makes a difference.
It does.**

William James

What people inspire you and why?

Day 23

**How vain it is to sit down to write
when you have not stood up to live.**

Henry David Thoreau

What makes you optimistic about your own future?

Day 24

**Sometimes one likes foolish people for their folly,
better than wise people for their wisdom.**

Elizabeth Gaskell

Write down three life lessons you've learned in recent years.

Day 25

The course of true love never did run smooth.

William Shakespeare

What are two or three things you can do to inspire other people?

Day 26

**The moment you doubt whether you can fly,
you cease forever to be able to do it.**

J. M. Barrie

Write down one or two you think are absolute self-confident. Now write
down all the qualities you have in common with him or her.

Day 27

Remember that very little is needed to make a happy life.

Marcus Aurelius

Write down a list with all the things that make you feel joyful.
Do one of those things today.

Day 28

If you look for perfection, you'll never be content.

Leo Tolstoy

What past experiences about your physical attractiveness
make you feel insecure?

What is one thing you can do to better deal with these insecurities?

Day 29

That it will never come again is what makes life so sweet.

Emily Dickinson

Write down a list of things you can do to increase your productivity. What is one thing you can do this week to increase your productivity?

Day 30

Hope is a waking dream.

Aristotle

Name three past experiences where you underestimated yourself, and surprised yourself.

_____
_____
_____
_____
_____
_____
_____
_____
_____
_____
_____
_____
_____
_____
_____
_____
_____
_____
_____
_____
_____
_____
_____

Day 31

Always forgive your enemies; nothing annoys them so much.

Oscar Wilde

Is the way you set goals and your to-do-lists a source of energy?
Or is it giving you stress?

_____
_____
_____
_____
_____
_____
_____
_____
_____
_____
_____
_____
_____
_____
_____
_____
_____
_____
_____
_____
_____
_____
_____
_____
_____
_____
_____
_____

Day 32

To love another person is to see the face of God.
Victor Hugo

What habits you have don't empower your life?

Day 33

"Chaos often breeds life, when order breeds habit."

Henry Adams

What habits do you have that empower your life?
How could you integrate one more empowering habit?

Day 34

**I do not want people to be very agreeable,
as it saves me the trouble of liking them a great deal.**

Jane Austen

What do you need now to feel more self-confident?

Day 35

When the heart is at ease, the body is healthy.

Chinese proverb

What is the influence of your health on feeling self-confident?

Day 36

**I am not afraid of storms,
for I am learning how to sail my ship.**

Louisa May Alcott

Write down a list of small things you can do to improve your health.
What is one thing you can do this week to improve your health?

Day 37

**Never close your lips to those
whom you have already opened your heart.**

Charles Dickens

How much time do you waste each day by worrying and overthinking?

What would happen if you used this time to think constructively about
problems and working on your desired life?

Day 38

**Respect was invented to cover the empty place
where love should be.**

Leo Tolstoy

What has pessimism brought you so far?

Day 39

Never tell the truth to people who are not worthy of it.

Mark Twain

In what ways do your fears, insecurities and social anxiety's
have anything to do with seeking validation?

Day 40

"You'll never find a rainbow if you're looking down."
Charlie Chaplin

What past experiences in your love life make you feel insecure?
What are three things you can do to better deal with these insecurities?

Day 41

Taking a new step, uttering a new word, is what people fear most.

Fyodor Dostoevsky

Pick your three biggest worries and ask yourself the following questions:

Do these worries are within my control?
From 1 to 10 how likely is it that these worries are actually going to happen?
And what can you do when the worst-case scenario comes to reality?

Day 42

Believe nothing you hear, and only one half that you see.

Edgar Allan Poe

In what situations do you most feel the need to be in control?

Day 43

**Music expresses that which cannot be put into words
and that which cannot remain silent.**

Victor Hugo

What is the influence of your financial situation on feeling self-confident?

Day 44

If there were no thunder, men would have little fear of lightning.

Jules Verne

Write down a list of things you can do to improve your financial situation.
What is one thing you can do this week to improve your financial situation?

_____

_____

_____

_____

_____

_____

_____

_____

_____

_____

_____

_____

_____

_____

_____

_____

_____

_____

_____

_____

_____

_____

_____

_____

_____

_____

_____

Day 45

One wondering thought pollutes the day.

Mary Shelley

How is people pleasing hurting your self-confidence?

Day 46

It is bizarre to treat all differences as oppositions.

Kate Chopin

What can other people learn from you when it comes to finances?

Day 47

Never stand begging for that which you have the power to earn.

Miguel de Cervantes Saavedra

What is holding you back the most to express yourself fully?

Day 48

We are like chameleons, we take our hue and the color of our moral character, from those who are around us.

John Locke

How do authenticity and self-confidence go hand in hand?

Day 49

**It is a narrow mind which cannot look at a subject
from various points of view.**

George Eliot

What is the influence of your social life on feeling self-confident?

Day 50

**I don't know half of you half as well as I should like;
and I like less than half of you half as well as you deserve.**

J.R.R. Tolkien

Write down a list of seven things you can do to improve your social life.
What is one thing you can do this week to improve your social life?

Day 51

**Attachment is the great fabricator of illusions;
reality can be obtained only by someone who is detached.**

Simone Weil

Write down seven things why you are worth loving.

Day 52

**In silence, I hear my special song,
composed on the wings of this universe.**

Zen Mirrors

Do you feel life is treating you fair?
Why or why not?

Day 53

We learn not in the school, but in life.

Lucius Annaeus Seneca

What do you frequently do to escape unpleasant situations?

Day 54

Live in the sunshine, swim the sea, drink the wild air.
Ralph Waldo Emerson

What are your personal boundaries?
Do people often cross them?
Why or why not?

Day 55

**We are like islands in the sea, separate on the surface
but connected in the deep.**

William James

What has being good enough in the opinion of others brought you so far?

Day 56

**When we love, we always strive to become better than we are.
When we strive to become better than we are, everything around us
becomes better too.**

Paulo Coelho

What is the influence of your love life on feeling self-confident?

Day 57

Dreams are the touchstones of our characters.

Henry David Thoreau

Write down a list of small things you can do to improve your love life.
What is one thing you can do this week to improve your love life?

Day 58

**If you are distressed by anything external,
the pain is not due to the thing itself, but to your estimate of it;
and this you have the power to revoke at any moment.**

Marcus Aurelius

How many of the things you worried about
did actually exactly happen the way you thought they might?

Day 59

But the future must be met, however stern and iron it be.
Elizabeth Gaskell

What is the biggest insecurity you have right now?
What is one small thing you can do today to improve that situation or
reduce your insecurity?

Day 60

I like this place and could willingly waste my time in it.

William Shakespeare

Which one of your biggest flaws do you like to rationalize the most and why?

Day 61

**Not knowing when the dawn will come
I open every door.**

Emily Dickinson

Write down a long list of compliments you have received over the years.

Day 62

**Educating the mind without educating the heart
is no education at all.**

Aristotle

How can you use your sexual energy to improve your productivity
and self-confidence?

_____

_____

_____

_____

_____

_____

_____

_____

_____

_____

_____

_____

_____

_____

_____

_____

_____

_____

_____

_____

_____

_____

_____

_____

Day 63

We are all in the gutter, but some of us are looking at the stars.

Oscar Wilde

What is one small action you can take today,
that will make you proud of yourself?

Day 64

The distance is nothing when one has a motive.

Jane Austen

Make an agreement to face one fear this week. Take a small step to decrease the influence of this particular fear in your life. You can either take action by simply feeling the fear and doing it anyway. Or by putting yourself in the feared situation and noticing what this fear actually is.

Example: You feel an almost deathly fear of talking to strangers. Option 1: Go to a shopping mall and, despite the fear, ask three persons for directions or the time.

Option 2: Go to a bar or an event and just notice what feelings and thoughts come up. Do you feel tightness in your stomach? Your throat? What thoughts are rushing to your mind? Don't you want to intrude? Don't you know what to say? Just pay attention to what is coming up. You don't necessarily have to take action. When you're at home write down your reflection of your night out.

Awareness alone could give you just enough courage to act despite fear.

Day 65

**The power of finding beauty in the humblest things
makes home happy and life lovely.**

Louisa May Alcott

What has underestimating yourself brought you so far?

Day 66

After all, the true seeing is within.
George Eliot

What is your definition of authenticity?

Day 67

**The power of finding beauty in the humblest things
makes home happy and life lovely.**

Louisa May Alcott

If you would act as your most courageous and fearless self,
what is the one thing you would do today?

Day 68

"As we express our gratitude, we must never forget that the highest appreciation is not to utter words, but to live by them."

John F. Kennedy

Write down two or three things you can do easily
that most other people find challenging?

Day 69

Facts are the enemy of truth.

Miguel de Cervantes Saavedra

What is your favorite strategy to deal with criticism?
Why do you use this strategy?

_____

_____

_____

_____

_____

_____

_____

_____

_____

_____

_____

_____

_____

_____

_____

_____

_____

_____

_____

_____

_____

_____

_____

_____

_____

_____

Day 70

The art of being wise is knowing what to overlook.

William James

Today release all your negative thoughts, worries,
and insecurities on paper.

Day 71

Absolutely unmixed attention is prayer.

Simone Weil

Write down a list of things you can do to enhance your personal style.
What is one thing you can do this week to feel more attractive?

_____

_____

_____

_____

_____

_____

_____

_____

_____

_____

_____

_____

_____

_____

_____

_____

_____

_____

_____

_____

_____

_____

Day 72

**It's the grown-up who disciplines himself,
that can safely see the world as a child.**

Zen Mirrors

What is the influence of being productive on feeling self-confident?

Day 73

Hold up your head! You were not made for failure, you were made for victory. Go forward with a joyful confidence.

George Eliot

What past experiences in your career make you feel insecure?
What is one thing you can do to better deal with these insecurities?

Day 74

No medicine cures what happiness cannot.

Gabriel García Márquez

What is the one thing you love doing that makes you happy,
but you neglect it because you're afraid of what others would think?

Day 75

**If you wish to forget anything on the spot,
make a note that this thing is to be remembered.**

Edgar Allan Poe

Write down a list of strengths you have
when it comes to interacting with people?

Day 76

To love truth for truth's sake is the principal part of human perfection in this world, and the seed-plot of all other virtues.

John Locke

Write down ten of your most common anxieties
and then trade them in for appreciation.

Example: I feel anxious to mingle with my colleagues.

→

I am grateful for my job and the possibility to mingle with colleagues

Day 77

**Happiness does not depend on outward things,
but on the way we see them.**

Leo Tolstoy

How do you deal with taking responsibility
when something doesn't go your way?

Day 78

"I am a part of all that I have met."

Alfred Tennyson

Take a good look at your wardrobe, your makeup, haircut, perfume: does your physical appearance, including clothing represent who you really are? Try to make at least one small change this month with your appearance, that will increase your attractiveness in your own eyes.

Dare to take a little bit of a risk.

Day 79

A day wasted on others is not wasted on one's self.
Charles Dickens

What is your favorite strategy to deal with failures?
Why do you use this strategy?

Day 80

**If we go down into ourselves,
we find that we possess exactly what we desire.**

Simone Weil

What can other people learn from you when it comes to productivity?

Day 81

Nothing happens to anybody which he is not fitted by nature to bear.

Marcus Aurelius

What past experiences in social interactions make you feel insecure?
What are two or three things to do to better deal with these insecurities?

Day 82

**"But he who dares not grasp the thorn
Should never crave the rose."**

Anne Brontë

If you would act as your most courageous and fearless self for one week straight, what would happen? And what is the first thing you would do?

_____

_____

_____

_____

_____

_____

_____

_____

_____

_____

_____

_____

_____

_____

_____

_____

_____

_____

_____

_____

_____

_____

_____

_____

_____

Day 83

To live is so startling it leaves little time for anything else.

Emily Dickinson

What new aspects of yourself have you noticed over the past few months

Day 84

Patience is bitter, but its fruit is sweet.

Aristotle

What is your favorite strategy for avoiding difficult situations?
What's a better strategy?

Day 85

**Watch and pray, dear, never get tired of trying,
and never think it is impossible to conquer your fault.**

Louisa May Alcott

What patterns keep returning when it comes to speaking up for yourself?

Day 86

Adventure is not outside man; it is within.

George Eliot

What makes it most difficult for you to accept yourself truly and wholeheartedly?

Day 87

Character is like a tree and reputation its shadow.
The shadow is what we think it is and the tree is the real thing.

Abraham Lincoln

When was the last time you didn't tell the truth to protect your image?

Day 88

Fortune sides with him who dares.

Virgil

Is life short?
The one thing we know for sure tomorrow is NEVER a guarantee.

What risk should you actually take?

Day 89

The delicious breath of rain was in the air.

Kate Chopin

What one piece of advice would you give yourself, after 89 days of journaling? And what one message would you share with the world?

Day 90

**We are more often frightened than hurt;
and we suffer more from imagination than from reality.**

Lucius Annaeus Seneca

After three months of journaling,
what does being self-confident mean to you?
And who would you like to be three months from now?

About The Authors

We specialize in creating empowering, elegant & inspirational self-help journals. The power of journaling, of consistent self-reflection, is a scientifically proven habit that will benefit your life in truly astonishing ways. Mainly 90-Day or Yearly Journals, on various topics and for all types of people. Tools for self-reflection, gratitude & personal growth. We create each journal or workbook with the utmost care and the honest intention to give lasting benefit to our customers.

We hope to guide you through releasing limitations and discover your hidden potentials in all areas of life. And of course to give an enjoyable journaling experience. Step by step, to unlock the true you. Step by step, to a better world.

We'd love to hear your ideas, tips, and questions. Let us know at exercises21@yahoo.com

Other Books by 21 Exercises

Finding Undiscovered Me, A One-Year Self-Discovery Year
The 90-Days Gratitude Journal
The 365 Creativity Journal (coming soon)

And more.

See for a list of all of our other books our Amazon author page:

www.amazon.com/21-Exercises/e/B07RGJ1WVT/

THE SELF-CONFIDENCE JOURNAL

Follow us on Instagram
For promotions, giveaways and newest arrivals

Instagram: 21exercises_journals

Made in the USA
Middletown, DE
16 September 2022

10617206R00064